the To&Through project

UCHICAGO Consortium on School Research

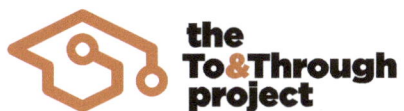

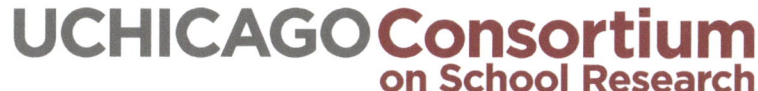

RESEARCH REPORT OCTOBER 2018

Hidden Risk

Changes in GPA across the Transition to High School

Alex Seeskin, Jenny Nagaoka, and Shelby Mahaffie

TABLE OF CONTENTS

1 Introduction

Chapter 1
3 Changes in Core GPA between the Eighth and Ninth Grades

Chapter 2
9 Non-Core GPA Declines across the Transition

Chapter 3
13 Course Failure and High School Graduation

Chapter 4
17 Implications

19 References

21 Appendices

The To&Through Project is a partnership between the University of Chicago's Urban Education Institute and the Network for College Success. The Project's mission is to use research, data, and professional learning to help more students get to and through high school and college:

- Research that illuminates what matters most for students' high school and college success
- Data that guides efforts to improve students' attainment of key milestones
- Professional Learning that helps translate research and data into improved practice

In collaboration with educators, policymakers, and communities, the To&Through Project aims to significantly increase the percentage of Chicago Public Schools freshmen who graduate from high school and go on to earn a college degree, and to share the learning from Chicago with education stakeholders across the country.

ACKNOWLEDGEMENTS

The authors gratefully acknowledge the many people who contributed to this report. Consortium Steering Committee members Gina Caneva, Megan Hougard, and Beatriz Ponce de León offered very thoughtful reviews as we finalized the narrative, and members of the To&Through advisory group gave us helpful feedback as we considered framing. We thank members of UChicago Consortium's research review group, particularly Elaine Allensworth, Julia Gwynne, and Kylie Klein, as well as our external reviewers, Eliza Moeller and Mary Ann Pitcher, for their helpful feedback. The UChicago Consortium's communications team, including Bronwyn McDaniel, Jessica Tansey, Jessica Puller, and Alida Mitau, as well as additional support from Katelyn Silva and Andrew Zou, were instrumental in the production of this report. Several people from CPS gave us feedback at various stages in the report process and we are especially grateful to Julia DeBettencourt, Eileen Hare, Liz Kirby, Sarah Dickson, and Jeff Broom for their partnership in providing context and feedback on implications. Other CPS central office and school-based practitioners gave us incredibly valuable feedback throughout: Anna Alvarado, Karen Keyes, Sara Kempner, Sarah Dickson, Amanda Hormanski, Wayne Issa, Gerald Morrow, Erin Galfer, Mary Beck, and Jasmine Juárez. We also thank Todd Rosenkranz, Marisa de la Torre, W. David Stevens, and Elaine Allensworth for doing the initial analysis and writing the 2014 report that provided the base for this report.

This report was supported by the Crown Family Philanthropies. We thank them for their support and collaboration on this project. The UChicago Consortium gratefully acknowledges the Spencer Foundation and the Lewis-Sebring Family Foundation, whose operating grants support the work of the UChicago Consortium, and also appreciates the support from the Consortium Investor Council that funds critical work beyond the initial research: putting the research to work, refreshing the data archive, seeding new studies, and replicating previous studies. Members include: Brinson Foundation, Chicago Community Trust, CME Group Foundation, Crown Family Philanthropies, Lloyd A. Fry Foundation, Joyce Foundation, Lewis-Sebring Family Foundation, McDougal Family Foundation, Osa Foundation, Polk Bros. Foundation, Robert McCormick Foundation, Spencer Foundation, Steans Family Foundation, and The Chicago Public Education Fund.

Cite as: Seeskin, A., Nagaoka, J., & Mahaffie, S. (2018). *Hidden risk: Changes in GPA across the transition to high school.* Chicago, IL: University of Chicago Consortium on School Research.

This report was produced by the UChicago Consortium's publications and communications staff: Bronwyn McDaniel, Director of Outreach and Communication; Jessica Tansey, Communications Manager; Jessica Puller, Communications Specialist; and Alida Birkeland Mitau, Development and Communications Coordinator.

Graphic Design: Jeff Hall Design
Photography: Eileen Ryan
Editing: Katelyn Silva, Jessica Puller, Jessica Tansey, and Andrew Zou

10.2018/PDF/jh.design@rcn.com

Introduction

A successful freshman year of high school lays the foundation for the path to college: ninth-grade grades are powerful indicators of high school graduation, college access, and college degree attainment.[1] However, the transition from eighth to ninth grade is a time when students' academic performance often declines. A 2014 report from the University of Chicago Consortium on School Research (UChicago Consortium) found that Chicago Public Schools (CPS) students who entered high school in 2008 saw their average overall GPAs fall by more than one-half of a point between the eighth and ninth grades as a result of significant declines in both attendance and study habits.[2]

This report explores how CPS students' grades declined during the transition to high school in more detail, and it considers how both eighth- and ninth-grade grades have changed since the original report was written. It examines GPA declines in arts and PE/health grades in addition to grades in the core subject areas, and it breaks down these declines by race/ethnicity, gender, and eighth-grade achievement and looks at how these patterns vary across schools. It also explores the relationships between failures in ninth-grade core and non-core courses, credit accumulation, and high school graduation. The report concludes by providing implications for high schools of the patterns in course performance and their relationship to high school graduation.

As students move from elementary to high school, they experience significant disruptions to their academic support networks, social relationships, and daily routines. Ninth-graders must adjust to new academic environments and expectations, and they are likely to receive less personal attention from teachers and other school staff.[3] Research suggests that developmental challenges associated with the high school transition lead to declines in students' social-emotional well-being, school connectedness, and self-perception.[4] Following the transition, students experience increased symptoms of depression,[5] have fewer friends at school,[6] and are less likely to believe that they will attend college.[7]

Noncognitive factors like these impact students' academic achievement through effects on their attendance, study habits, and other academic behaviors.[8] Students' attendance declines precipitously between the eighth and ninth grades. In 2014, researchers at the UChicago Consortium found that the average ninth-grader accrued 21.4 unexcused absent days—nearly four times as many unexcused absences as the same students had on average in eighth grade—and that ninth-graders were less likely than eighth-graders to report that they study for tests, make time for homework, and prioritize schoolwork.[9] The 2014 study concluded that more than 85 percent of the decline in CPS students'

---

1 Allensworth & Clark (2018); Bowen, Chingos, & McPherson (2009); Camara & Echternacht (2000); Easton, Johnson, & Sartain (2017); Geiser & Santelices (2007); Roderick, Nagaoka, & Allensworth (2006).
2 Rosenkranz, de la Torre, Stevens, & Allensworth (2014).
3 Benner (2011); Rosenkranz et al. (2014).
4 Benner (2011); Benner & Graham (2009); Felmlee, McMillan, Rodis, & Osgood (2018); Andrew & Flashman (2017); Rosenkranz et al. (2014); Farrington et al. (2012).
5 Benner & Graham (2009).
6 Felmlee et al. (2018).
7 Andrew & Flashman (2017).
8 Farrington et al. (2012).
9 Rosenkranz et al. (2014).

math and English performance between the eighth and ninth grades could be explained by changes in students' attendance and self-reported academic effort, and that almost none of the gap could be attributed to changes in the difficulty of their coursework.[10]

Over the past decade, CPS has paid close attention to the transition to high school and has made significant progress in improving students' course performance in ninth grade.[11] Schools have been especially successful in reducing the frequency of ninth-grade failures in core courses, defined in this report as courses in math, English, science, and social studies.[12] This progress is demonstrated by improvements in high schools' Freshman OnTrack rates, which measure the proportion of first-time freshmen who accumulate at least five credits and fail no more than one semester of a core course during their freshman year. Freshman OnTrack is a strong predictor of high school graduation and is an important accountability metric for CPS high schools.[13] Since 2009, the overall Freshman OnTrack rate for CPS students has increased by 23 percentage points, from 66 percent to 88 percent in 2017.[14] This increase is the result of both improvements in incoming students' level of preparation[15] and targeted efforts by high schools to prevent ninth-grade course failure.[16]

Although freshman failure rates have improved, most CPS students continued to see significant declines in their GPA between the eighth and ninth grades. These persistent declines suggest a need for additional investment in supporting students during the transition to high school. In this report, we explore ninth-grade GPA declines and failure rates across different subject areas and student subgroups in order to identify areas where additional work may be necessary to minimize declines in course performance across the transition to high school for all students.

---

10 Rosenkranz et al. (2014).
11 Easton et al. (2017); Roderick, Kelley-Kemple, Johnson, & Beechum (2014).
12 This definition of core courses differs slightly from the definition of core courses that CPS used for the 2018-19 school year. For the purposes of this report, core courses include only courses in subjects that have been used to calculate students' on-track status in the past. Moving forward, arts courses, including courses in visual arts, music, and drama, will also be classified as core courses by CPS. The Freshman OnTrack indicator currently includes only math, English, science, and social studies in its definition of courses, and does not include arts.
13 Allensworth (2013).
14 Nagaoka, Seeskin, & Coca (2017).
15 Allensworth, Healey, Gwynne & Crespin (2016).
16 Roderick et al. (2014).

CHAPTER 1

Changes in Core GPA between the Eighth and Ninth Grades

Ninth-grade course performance in CPS in the four core subject areas included in the Freshman OnTrack metric—math, English, science, and social studies—has increased steadily over the past few years.[17] Between 2012 and 2017, the average ninth-grade core GPA increased 0.40 GPA points, from 2.18 to 2.58, the rough equivalent of going from a C+ to a B- (see Figure 1).[18] Simultaneously, trends in eighth-grade core GPA increased between 2012 and 2017, from 2.52 to 2.89. Yet students' GPAs continue to decline from eighth to ninth grade. In 2012, the decline was 0.34 points and in 2017, the decline was 0.31 points.

In each of the four core subject areas, the 2016–17 ninth-grade cohort saw an average decline in their grades of approximately one-third of a letter grade. Average GPA declines between the eighth and ninth grades were of the smallest magnitude in math (-0.26 points), where students earned the lowest grades in eighth grade, and of the largest magnitude in English (-0.38 points), where students earned the highest grades in eighth grade (see Figure 2).

Students at all levels of prior achievement saw declines in their average core grades between the eighth and ninth grades, and students with high eighth-grade

FIGURE 1

Students' Core GPAs Continued to Decline across the High School Transition, Despite Steady Improvement in Both Eighth- and Ninth-Grade Core Grades

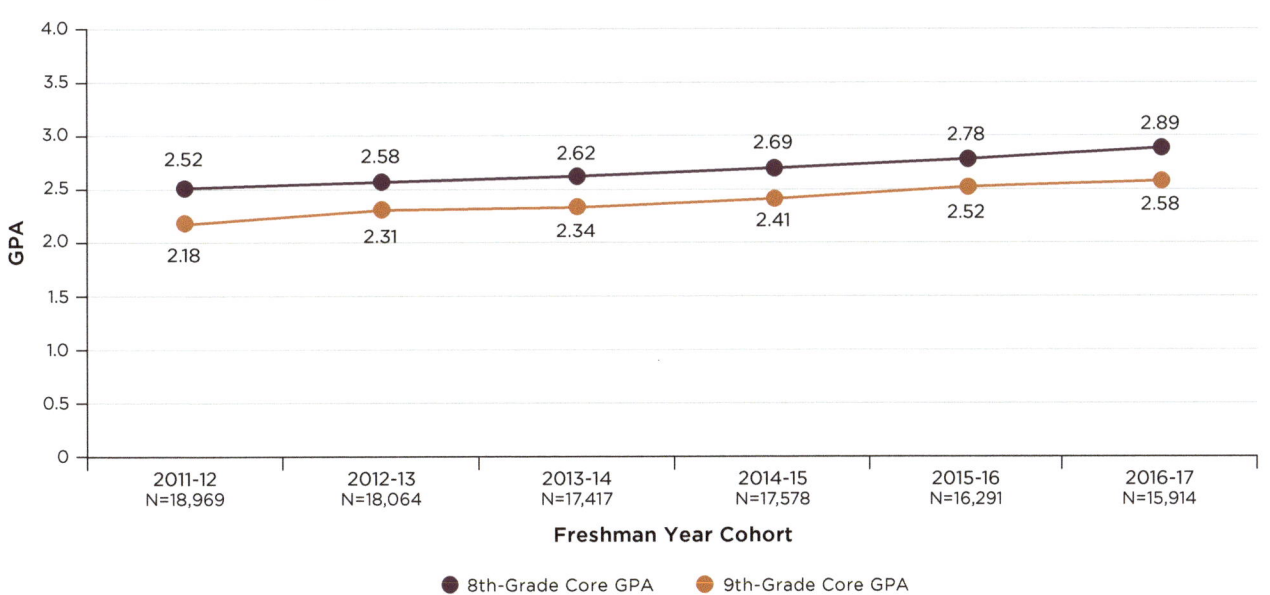

Note: Core courses are defined in this analysis as courses in math, English, social studies, and science. Students were included in this analysis only if their grade data was available for both eighth and ninth grades. This excludes students who attended a charter school for the duration of either their eighth-grade or ninth-grade school year. For more information, see Appendix A.

---

17 The analysis in this report used only grade data from non-charter schools. For more information, see Appendix A.
18 To calculate students' core GPAs, we averaged together all first and second semester grades in English, math, science, and social studies, assigning a value of 4.0 to As, 3.0 to Bs, 2.0 to Cs, 1.0 to Ds, and 0 to Fs, and gave no special weighting to honors, AP, or IB classes.

FIGURE 2

Students' Grades Fell Around One-Third of a Letter Grade in Each of the Core Subjects between the Eighth and Ninth Grades

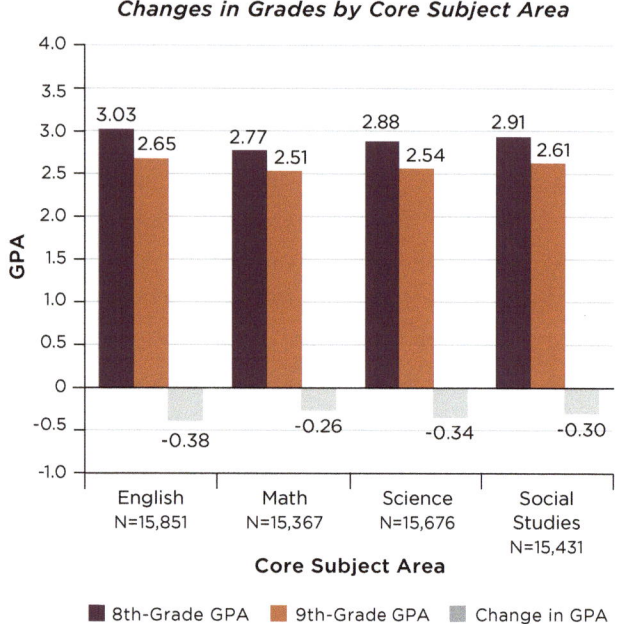

Changes in Grades by Core Subject Area

■ 8th-Grade GPA ■ 9th-Grade GPA ■ Change in GPA

Note: For each subject, students were included only if they received at least one grade in that subject in eighth grade during school year 2015-16 and at least one grade in that subject in ninth grade during school year 2016-17. Charter students were not included. For more information, see Appendix A.

grades and test scores were especially likely to see large declines (**see Figure 3**). On average, the students who earned eighth-grade core GPAs above 3.5 saw their core grades fall about one-half a point, from an A/A- to a B+. Students with low eighth-grade grades generally continued to earn low grades in ninth grade. Students who earned below a 2.0 core GPA in eighth grade continued to earn mostly Ds and Fs in ninth grade, seeing their core GPAs increase only 0.12 points as they moved to high school.

This pattern generally held for students with different levels of performance on eighth-grade standardized tests. Higher-achieving students, defined as those meeting or exceeding NWEA reading proficiency standards in eighth grade, saw their core grades fall slightly more than one-third of a letter grade between the eighth and ninth grades (**see Figure 4**).[19] On average, the core GPAs of students exceeding NWEA eighth-grade reading proficiency standards fell from a A-/B+ in eighth grade to a B in ninth grade, and the core GPAs of those meeting standards fell from a B to a B-/C+. The students who earned the lowest eighth-grade NWEA reading proficiency scores received low grades on average in eighth grade and continued to receive low grades in ninth grade, with their core GPAs starting at a C average in eighth grade and falling an additional 0.08 points on average by the end of ninth grade.

For the most part, students of different race/ethnicity and gender groups saw average core GPA declines of relatively similar magnitudes between the eighth and ninth grades despite having earned very different average GPAs in eighth grade (**see Figure 5**). Black and Latina young women saw the largest average declines in core GPA between the eighth and ninth grades, of 0.40 and 0.35 points, respectively. However, the impact of declines in GPA across the transition to high school may be most critical for Black and Latino young men, who saw declines nearly as large as those of their female peers despite having entered high school with significantly lower average eighth-grade GPAs. On average, Black young men entered high school with an eighth-grade core GPA of just 2.46, meaning that the decline of an additional one-third of a point in GPA between the eighth and ninth grades resulted in an average ninth-grade GPA of 2.12, or a C average. Asian students saw average declines of significantly smaller magnitude than their peers—0.18 points for Asian young men and 0.15 for Asian young women.

High-achieving Black and Latino students were especially likely to suffer large declines in core GPA during the transition to high school (**see Figure 6**). Among students with high eighth-grade core GPAs, Black students saw much larger declines in core GPA across the transition to high school than their peers with similar eighth-grade grades. For example, the average White student who earned an eighth-grade core GPA between 3.0 and 3.5 saw their core GPA decline by only 0.27 points between the eighth and ninth grades,

---

19 A similar pattern held across NWEA math proficiency categories, though the number of eighth-grade students exceeding standards in math (2,997) was lower than the number of students exceeding standards in reading and the average eighth-grade core GPA for these students (3.61) was slightly higher than that for students exceeding standards in reading.

FIGURE 3

On Average, Students with Higher Eighth-Grade Core GPAs Saw Larger Core GPA Declines than their Peers across the Transition to High School

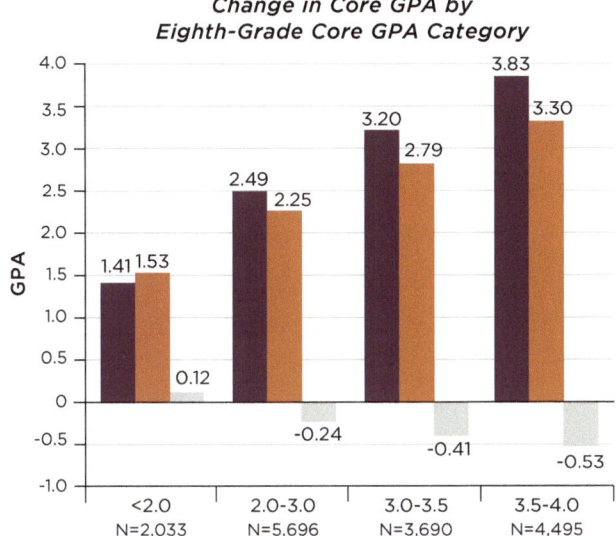

Note: Students were included only if they received grades in eighth grade during school year 2015-16 and in ninth grade during school year 2016-17. Charter students were not included. For more information, see Appendix A.

FIGURE 4

On Average, Students with Higher Test Scores in Eighth Grade Saw Larger Core GPA Declines than their Peers across the Transition to High School

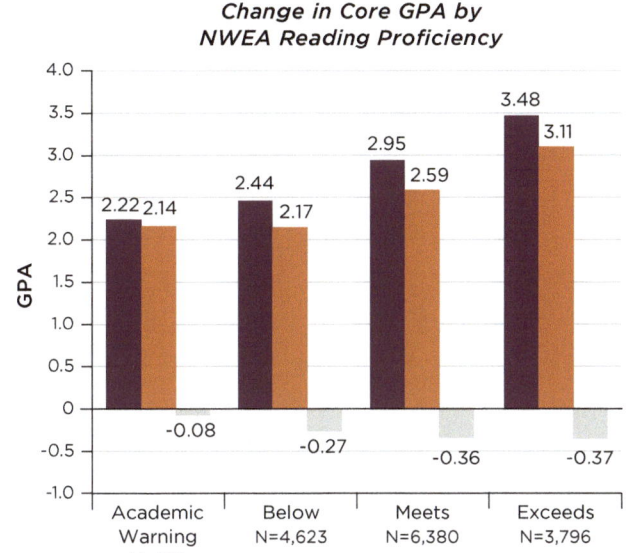

Note: These statistics included only members of the 2016-17 CPS ninth-grade cohort for whom both eighth-grade NWEA scores and eighth- and ninth-grade grades were available. This excludes students who attended a charter school for the duration of either their eighth-grade or ninth-grade school year. For more information, see Appendix A.

FIGURE 5

Students of Different Race/Ethnicity Groups Entered High School with Different Average Eighth-Grade GPAs but Saw Average GPA Declines of Somewhat Similar Magnitude

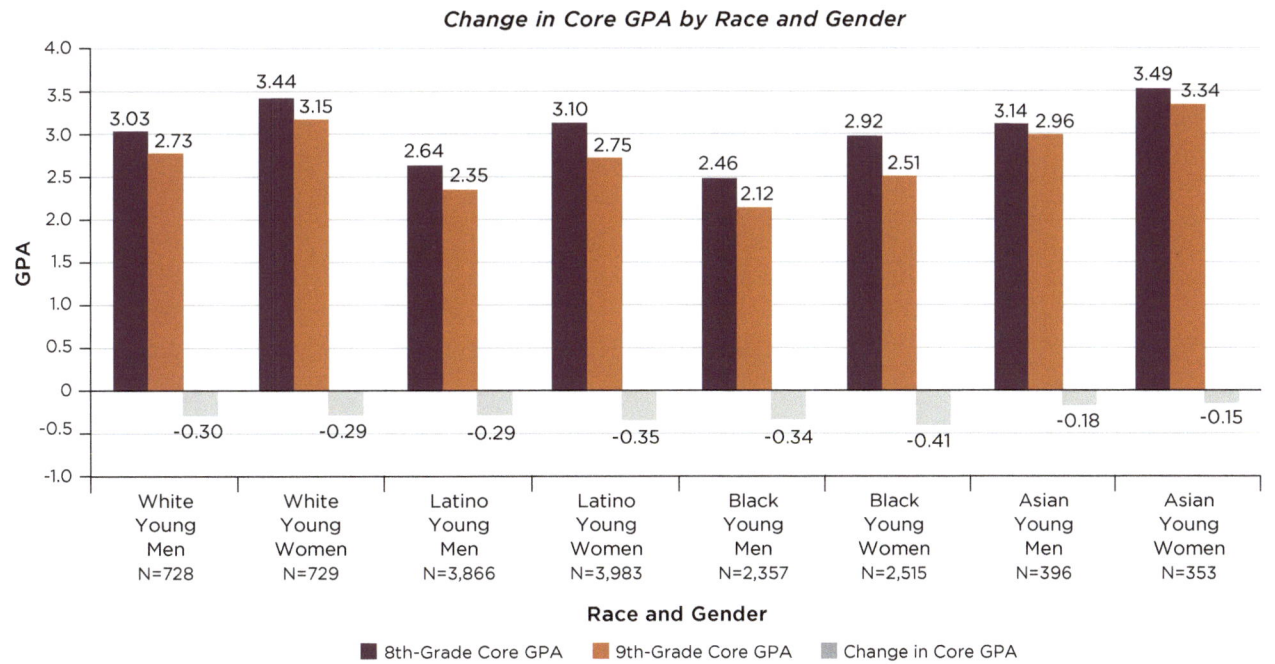

Note: These statistics included only members of the 2016-17 CPS freshman cohort for whom both eighth- and ninth-grade grades were available. This excludes students who attended a charter school for the duration of either their eighth-grade or ninth-grade school year. For more information, see Appendix A.

FIGURE 6

On Average, High-Achieving Black Students Saw the Largest Declines in Core GPA between the Eighth and Ninth Grades

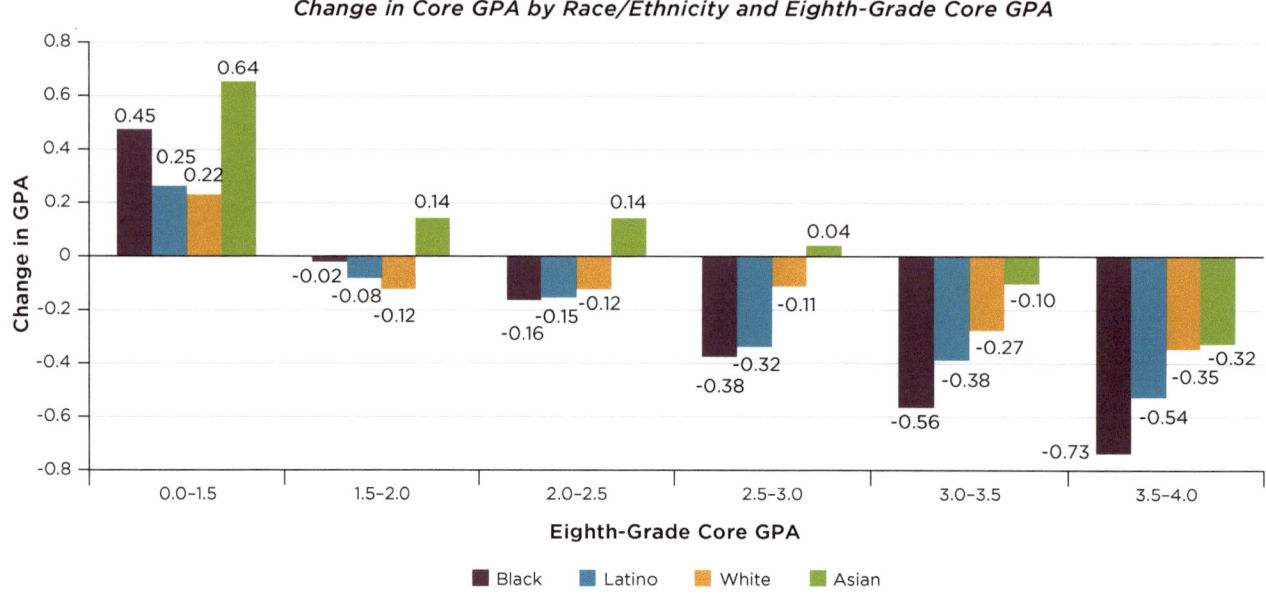

Change in Core GPA by Race/Ethnicity and Eighth-Grade Core GPA

Note: These statistics included only members of the 2016–17 CPS freshman cohort for whom both eighth- and ninth-grade grades were available. This excludes students who attended a charter school for the duration of either their eighth-grade or ninth-grade school year. For more information, see Appendix A.

but the average Black student in the same achievement category saw their core GPA decline by 0.56 points. This pattern held for all students with GPAs above 2.5: on average, high- and middle-achieving Black students saw declines at least twice as large as those of their White peers with similar eighth-grade core GPAs during the transition to high school.

These district-level averages masked considerable variation in patterns across individual high schools (**see Figure 7**). Of the 64 CPS high schools with at least 20 Black students in their 2016–17 freshman cohort, 17 schools saw their Black students lose more than 0.5 points in core GPA on average between the eighth and ninth grades, while 14 saw their Black students improve their GPAs, on average. The range of average declines in GPA across high schools was somewhat smaller for White and Asian students. At each of the 12 high schools with at least 20 Asian students in their 2016–17 freshman cohort, the average Asian student's core GPA changed less than 0.5 GPA points between the eighth and ninth grades. The same was true for the average White student at 16 of the 17 high schools with at least 20 White students.

Black and Latino students in selective enrollment high schools tended to see especially large declines in GPA during the transition to high school. At five of the eight selective enrollment schools with at least 20 Black students in their freshman cohort, the average Black students' GPA declined more than two-thirds of a letter grade between the eighth and ninth grades. The schools where Black and Latino students saw large gains in core GPA were primarily schools whose incoming students received low grades in eighth grade. Of the 14 high schools where the average Black student's GPA increased between the eighth and ninth grades, 13 were schools whose incoming freshman classes earned average GPAs below 2.5 in eighth grade. However, at other schools whose incoming classes earned average GPAs below 2.5, the average Black student saw as much as a 0.5 additional GPA point decline between the eighth and ninth grades. This type of variation suggests that high school environment plays an important role in determining whether students' course performance improves or declines as they move to high school.

FIGURE 7

Changes in Core GPAs Varied Widely across High Schools for Black and Latino Students

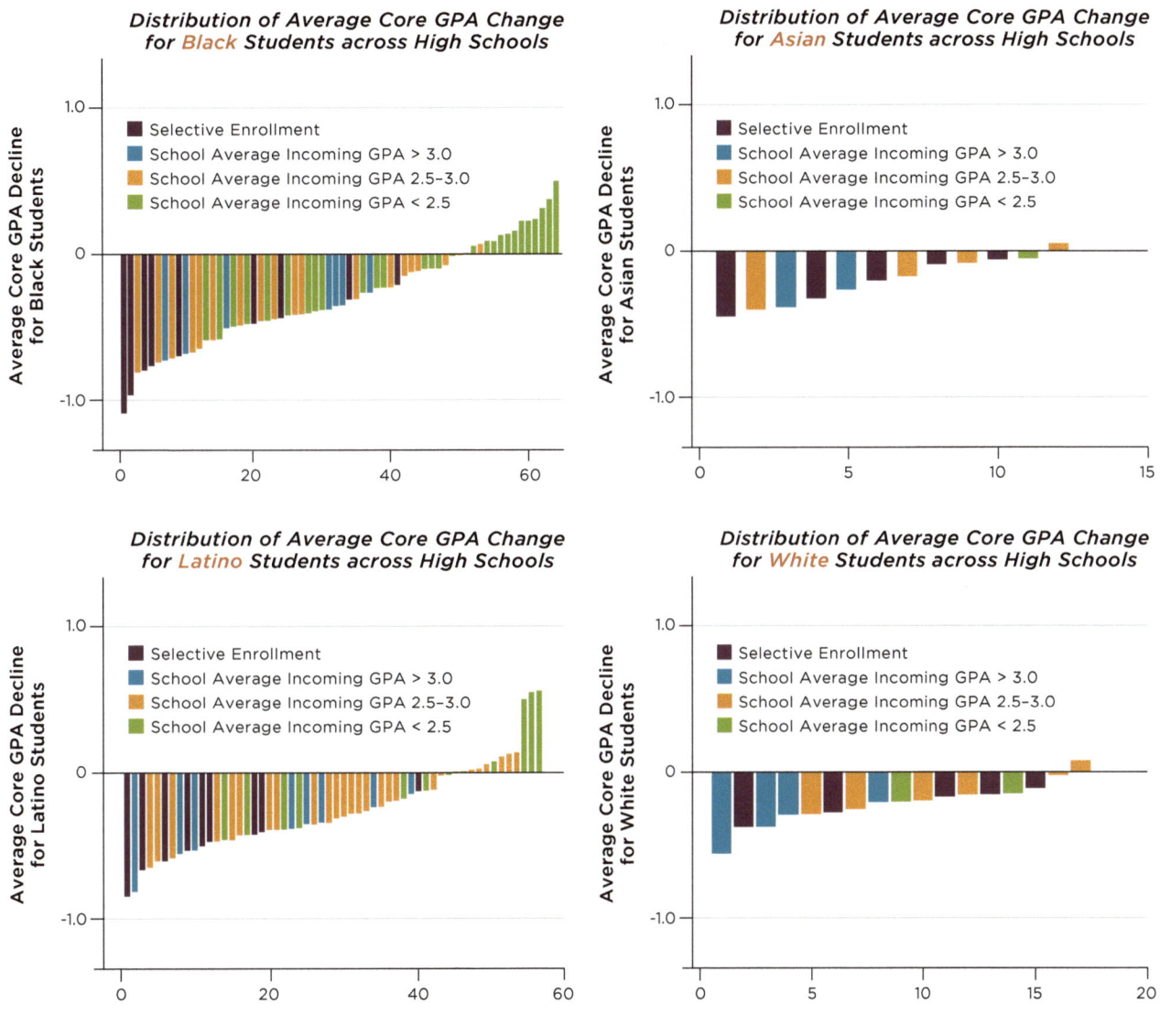

Note: For the graph associated with each race/ethnicity group, schools were included only if there were at least 20 students of that race/ethnicity in their 2016-17 freshman cohort. Charter high schools are not represented in these figures. Students who attended charter schools for the duration of eighth grade are not included in their high schools' averages because their eighth-grade grades are not available. For more information, see Appendix A.

CHAPTER 2

Non-Core GPA Declines Across the Transition

Previous Consortium research on the high school transition has focused primarily on students' declining grades in the core subject areas, in part because students' core grades in ninth grade largely determine their Freshman OnTrack status. However, declines in students' academic performance between the eighth and ninth grades are not limited to their grades in these four subjects. In fact, GPA declines in the two non-core subject areas common to both the eighth and ninth grades—PE/health and arts—greatly exceeded average declines in each of the core subject areas. In eighth grade, students earned mostly As and Bs in arts and PE/health, but in ninth grade, their grades in these subject areas fell to below a B. On average, students saw their grade decline by 0.81 points in PE/health between the eighth and ninth grades, and by 0.61 points in arts— declines much larger than the average core GPA decline of 0.33 points (see Figure 8).

This gap is so large in part because freshman grades in arts and PE/health have not seen the same growth as freshman grades in the core subjects over the past few years. While the average ninth-grade core course grade has increased 0.31 points since 2013, the average ninth-grade PE/health grade has increased only 0.18 points, and the average arts grade just 0.08 points (see Figure 9).

At the school level, while the freshman cohorts of some high schools now earn higher average core GPAs in ninth grade than they earned in eighth grade, the arts and PE/health grades of nearly all high schools' freshman cohorts declined significantly following the transition to high school. At 75 percent of CPS high schools, the average freshman earned a PE/health GPA more than 0.5 points lower than they earned in the eighth grade. The same is true of core GPA at only a handful of high schools (see Figure 10).

Nearly all students saw larger GPA declines in non-core courses than in core courses between the eighth and ninth grades, but non-core declines appeared to be

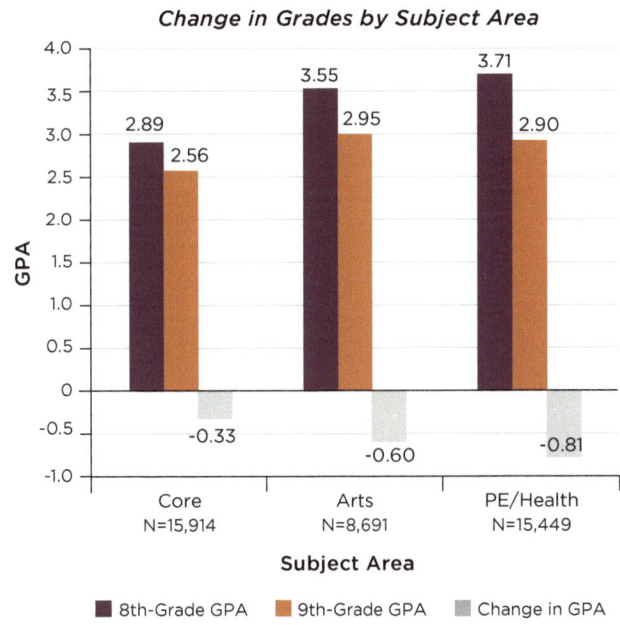

FIGURE 8

Declines in Students' Grades in Arts and PE/Health between the Eighth and Ninth Grades Greatly Exceeded Those in the Core Subject Areas

Note: For each subject area, students were included only if they received at least one grade in that subject area in eighth grade during school year 2015–16 and at least one grade in that subject area in ninth grade during school year 2016–17. This excludes students who attended a charter school for the duration of either their eighth-grade or ninth-grade school year. For more information, see Appendix A.

particularly disproportionate for the students at the highest risk of dropping out of high school. Students with low eighth-grade core GPAs saw very large declines in their grades in the non-core subject areas between the eighth and ninth grades. Ninth-graders who received a core GPA lower than 2.0 in the eighth grade saw their average PE/health grade decline by 1.39 points, from a B in eighth grade to a C- in ninth grade (see Figure 11). The same students lost, on average, more than a full letter grade in arts over the same period.

Black and Latino young men also saw especially large grade declines, on average, in the non-core subject areas. The arts grades of Black young men fell by more than three-quarters of a point between the eighth and ninth grades, and their PE/health grades fell a full point (see Figure 12).

FIGURE 9

Students' Grades in Arts and PE/Health Have Not Increased as Much as their Grades in Core Subjects in Either Eighth or Ninth Grade

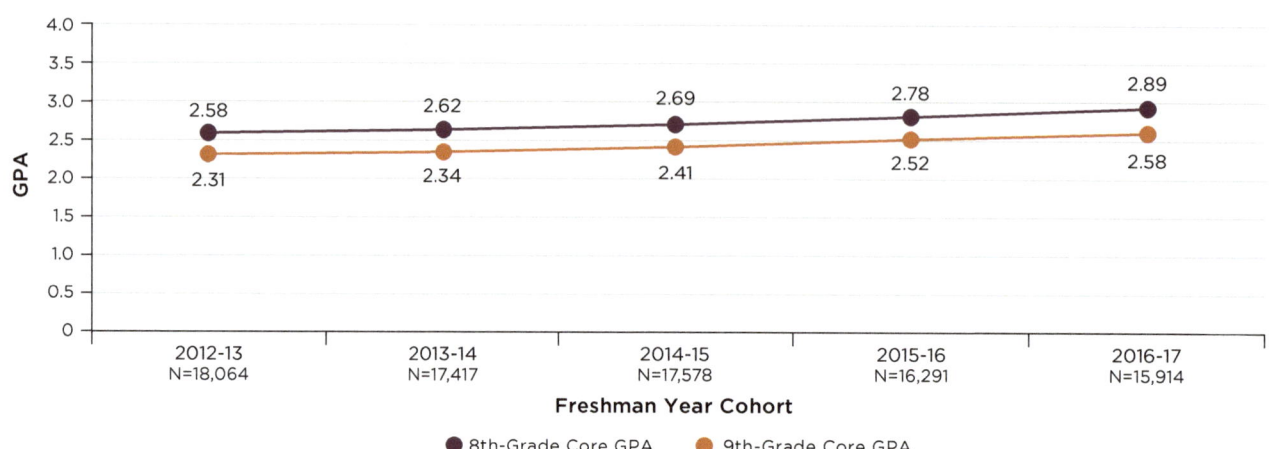

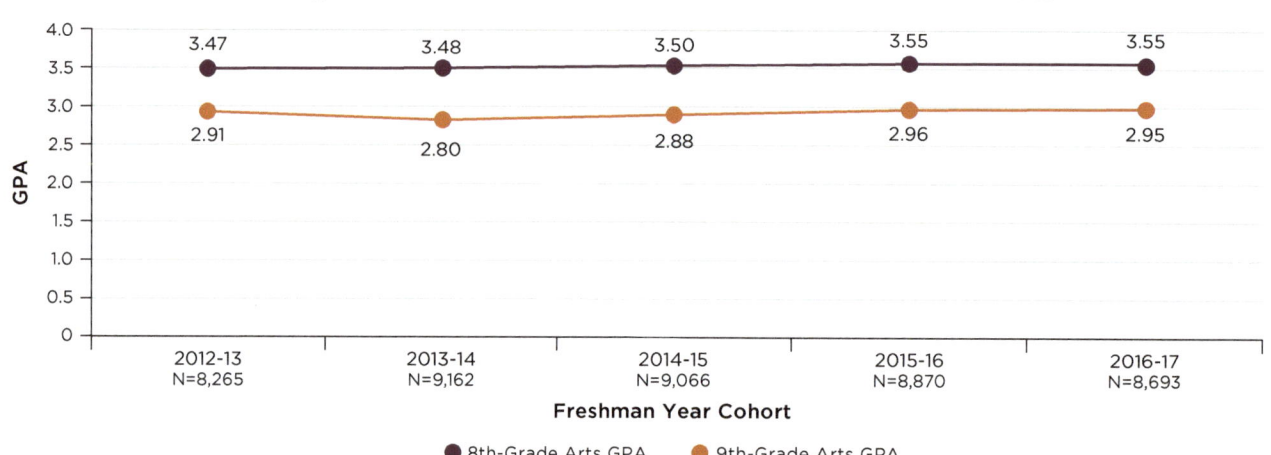

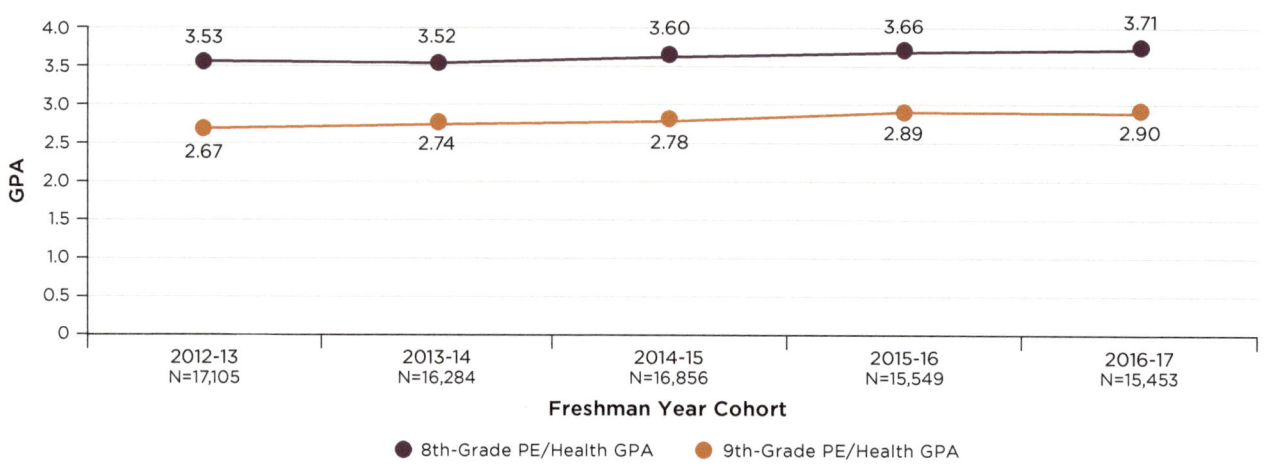

Note: For each subject area, students were included only if they received at least one grade in that subject area in eighth grade during school year 2015–16 and at least one grade in that subject area in ninth grade during school year 2016–17. This excludes students who attended a charter school for the duration of either their eighth-grade or ninth-grade school year. For more information, see Appendix A.

FIGURE 10

Students at Nearly All CPS High Schools Saw Significant Declines in PE/Health and Arts Grades between the Eighth and Ninth Grades

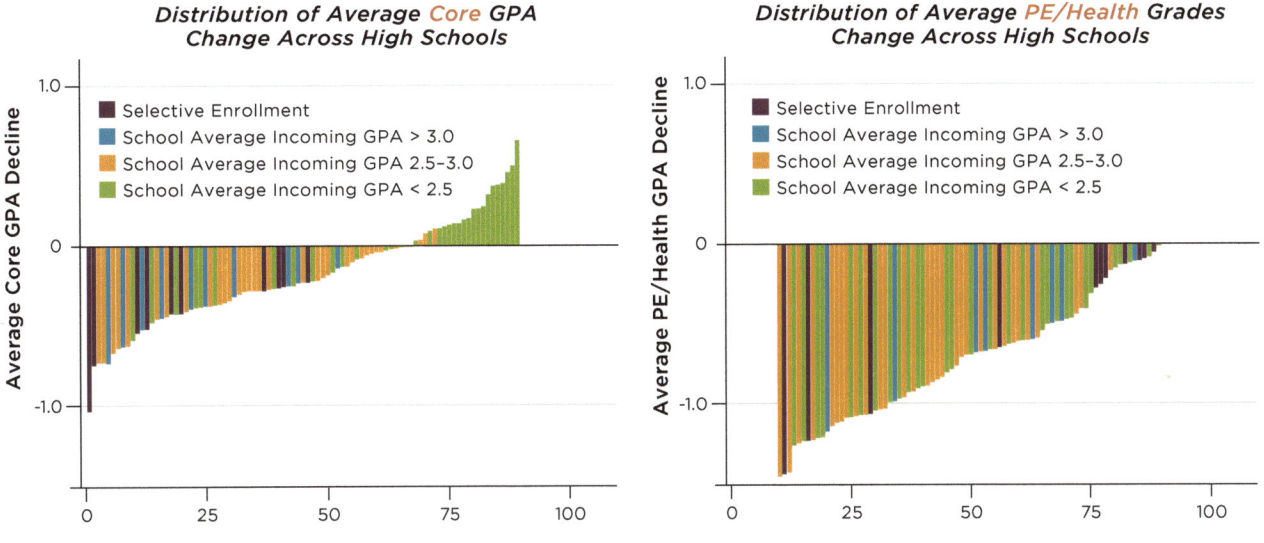

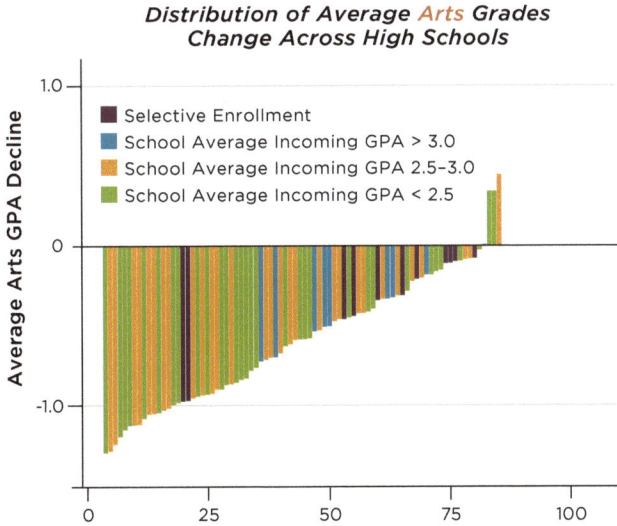

Note: For the graph associated with each race/ethnicity group, schools were included only if there were at least 20 students of that race/ethnicity in their 2016-17 freshman cohort. Charter high schools are not represented in these figures. Students who attended charter schools for the duration of eighth grade are not included in their high schools' averages because their eighth-grade grades are not available. For more information, see Appendix A.

UCHICAGO Consortium Research Report | Hidden Risk

FIGURE 11

Grade Declines in the Non-Core Subject Areas Were Especially Large for Students with Low Eighth-Grade Core GPAs

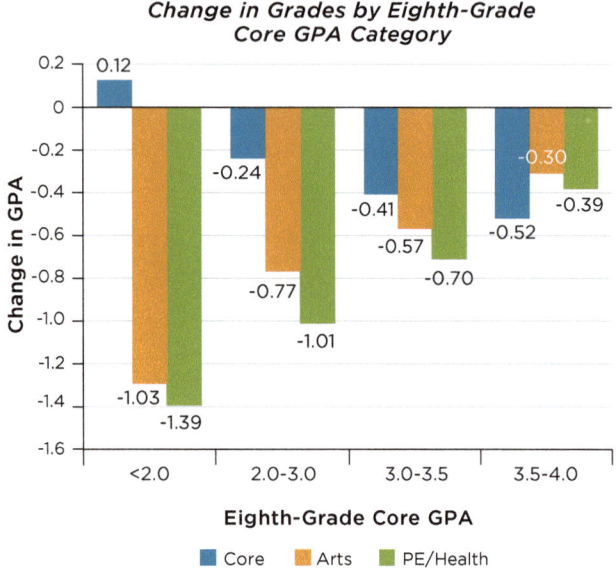

Note: For each subject area, students were included only if they received at least one grade in that subject area in eighth grade during school year 2015-16 and at least one grade in that subject area in ninth grade during school year 2016-17. This excludes students who attended a charter school for the duration of either their eighth-grade or ninth-grade school year. For more information, see Appendix A. For students' average incoming GPAs by subject and eighth grade GPA category, see Appendix B.

FIGURE 12

Black and Latino Young Men Saw by Far the Largest Average Grade Declines in PE/Health and Arts

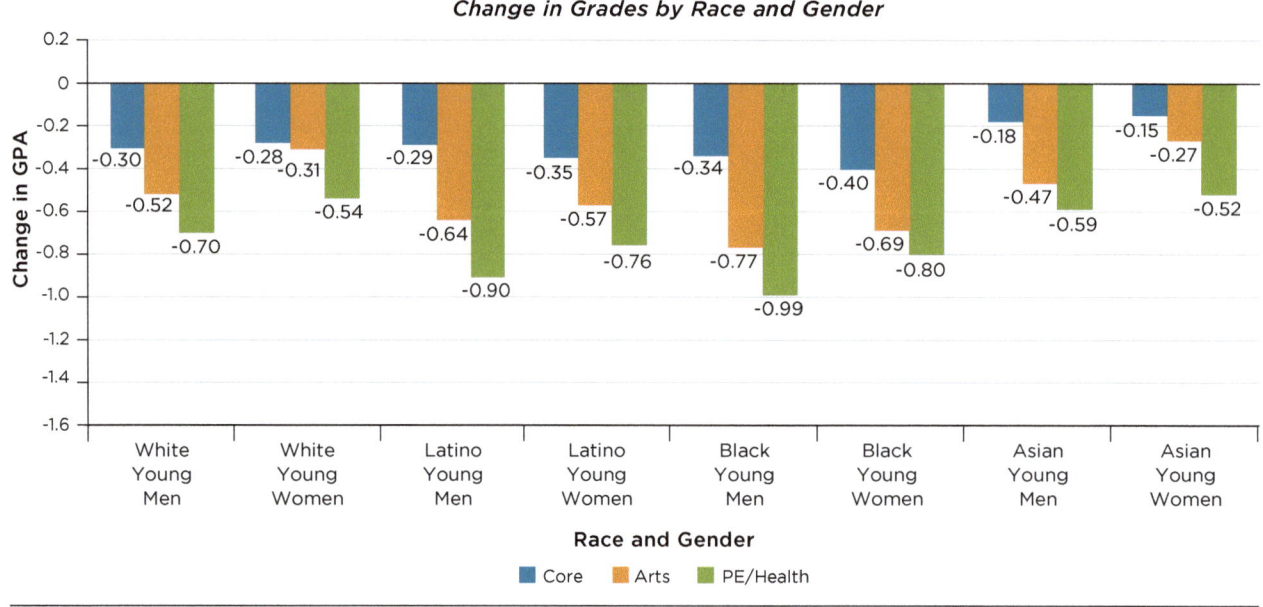

Note: For each subject area, students were included only if they received at least one grade in that subject area in eighth grade during school year 2015-16 and at least one grade in that subject area in ninth grade during school year 2016-17. This excludes students who attended a charter school for the duration of either their eighth-grade or ninth-grade school year. For more information, see Appendix A. For students' average incoming GPAs by subject and race/ethnicity and gender group, see Appendix B.

Chapter 2 | Non-Core GPA Declines across the Transition

CHAPTER 3

Course Failure and High School Graduation

Incremental improvements in ninth-grade grades are associated with better outcomes for students at all levels of achievement, but course failure is an especially powerful indicator of whether students will graduate.[20] Students who fail courses in ninth grade typically see their academic performance only further decline as they move through high school, and course failure often signals a broader disengagement from school in general.[21] Failure in any subject area and at any grade level presents threats for students' academic identity and sense of school belonging.[22] In high school, course failure also takes on an additional structural importance that doesn't exist in elementary school: when students fail courses in high school, they miss opportunities to earn credits that they must accumulate in order to keep pace to graduate from high school within four years.[23]

Unfortunately, failure rates increased considerably in all subject areas across the transition to high school. Failure rates in arts and PE/health showed especially significant increases: failures in PE and health were highly uncommon in the middle grades, but more than 1,200 students in the 2016–17 freshman cohort (8.2 percent) failed at least one semester of PE/health in the ninth grade, and almost 700 (4.3 percent) failed at least one semester of arts (see Figure 13).[24] In ninth grade, the proportion of students failing at least one semester of PE/health (8.2 percent) exceeded the proportion failing at least one semester of social studies (7.8 percent) and almost matched the proportion of students failing at least one semester of science (8.5 percent) and English (8.8 percent). Not all students who failed non-core courses during freshman year failed core courses

FIGURE 13

More Students Failed Courses in All Subject Areas in Ninth Grade than in Eighth Grade, but the Failure Rate in PE/Health Increased Most (2016-17 Freshman Cohort)

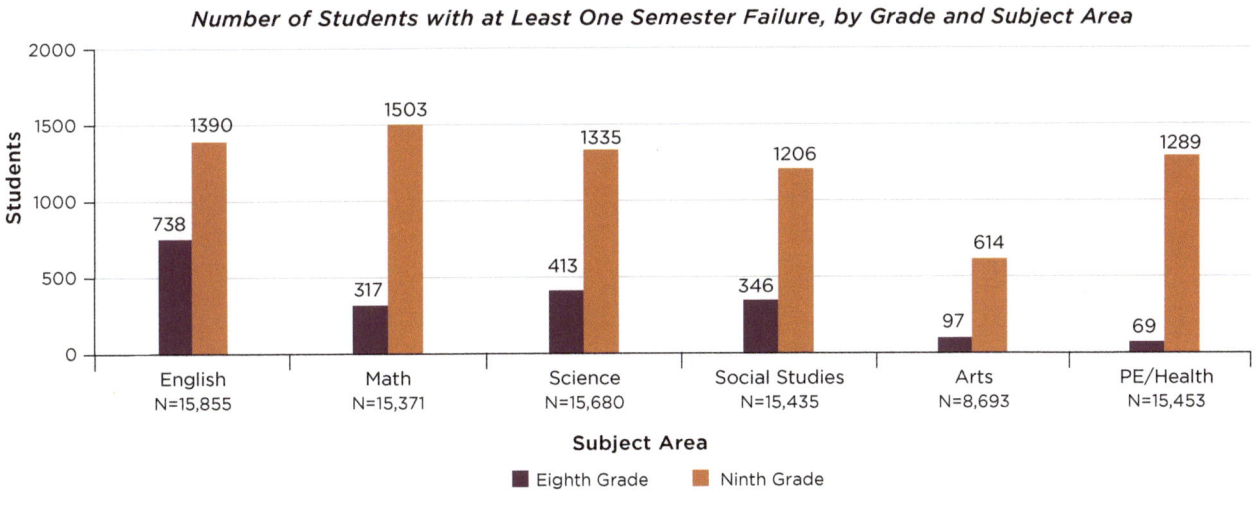

Note: For each subject area, students were included only if they received at least one grade in that subject area in eighth grade during school year 2015–16 and at least one grade in that subject area in ninth grade during school year 2016–17. This excludes students who attended a charter school for the duration of either their eighth-grade or ninth-grade school year. For more information, see Appendix A.

---

20 Easton et al. (2017); Roderick et al. (2014).
21 Roderick & Camburn (1999).
22 Farrington et al. (2012).
23 Farrington et al. (2012).

24 The number of students who failed an arts course was smaller than the number of students who failed a PE/health, in part, because fewer students took an arts course in ninth grade than took a PE/health course. For course failure rates by subject, see Appendix B, Table B.3 and Table B.4.

as well. More than 3,500 students in the 2011–14 freshman cohorts (6.7 percent of all ninth-graders) achieved an on-track status but failed at least one semester of a non-core course during their freshman year. Over the same time period, more than 2,400 ninth-graders passed all of their core courses but failed at least one semester of a non-core course.

Because students' Freshman OnTrack status is largely determined by the number of core courses they fail, schools' efforts to monitor freshman progress often focus on preventing course failure in the core subject areas. This work has contributed to significant improvements in ninth-grade failure rates. Ninth-grade failures have fallen in all subject areas since 2012, and failures in the core subjects have fallen most rapidly (**see Figure 14**).

However, for recent cohorts of CPS students, all course failures in ninth grade, regardless of subject area, were associated with large decreases in students' likelihood of graduating from high school. Among the 2011–14 freshman cohorts, an additional non-core failure and an additional core failure were associated with similar decreases in graduation rates for students with any given number of core and non-core failures. For example, the graduation rate for students with one core course failure and no other failures in ninth grade was 70 percent; for students with one non-core course failure and no other failures, the graduation rate was very similar, at 68 percent. Students who passed all their courses during ninth grade, meanwhile, had a 90 percent chance of graduating within four years (**see Table 1**). Nearly all students in the entire first two columns of Table 1—all those with either zero or one semester failure of a core course as first-time ninth-graders—earned an on-track status during their freshman year. However, their actual likelihoods of graduating differed significantly depending on the number of non-core courses they failed as first-time ninth-graders. For example, the 326 students who failed only one semester of a core course but failed two semesters of non-core courses likely received an on-track status in the ninth grade, but only 44 percent of them went on to graduate from high school within four years.

Graduation rates for students who accumulated different numbers of credits in ninth grade also highlight the importance of passing non-core courses in ninth grade. In addition to failing no more than one semester of a core class, to be on-track, ninth-graders also need to accumulate five total credits during their freshman year of high school. However, students who earned six or seven credits as ninth-graders were much more likely than students who earned only five credits to graduate from high school within four years (**see Figure 15**). For the 2013-14 freshman cohort, the 12,560 ninth-graders who accumulated at least seven credits (69.4 percent of students) had a four-year graduation rate of 89 percent, while the 798 (4.4 percent) of students who earned only

FIGURE 14

Failure Rates in the Core Subjects Have Fallen Significantly Since 2013 for Both Eighth- and Ninth-Grade Students

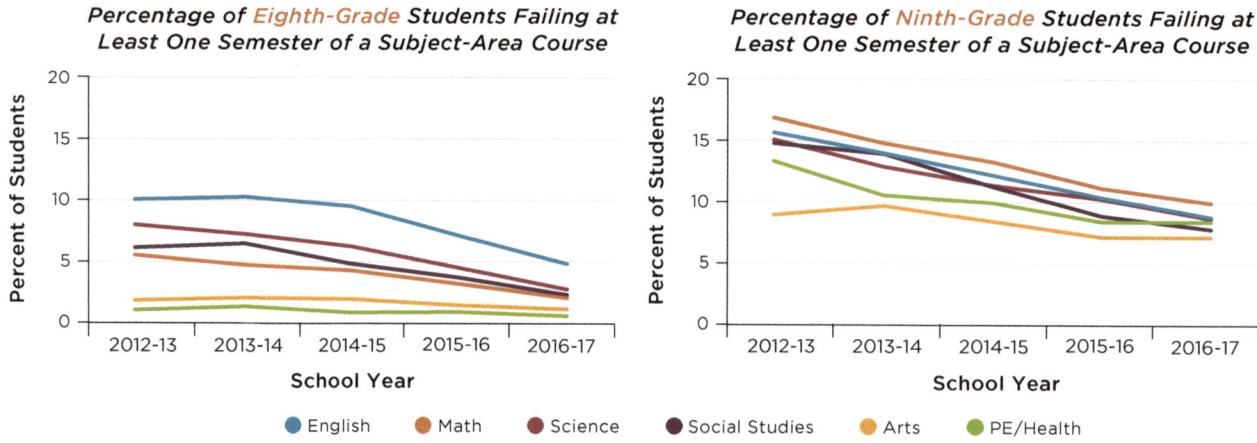

Note: For each subject area, students were included only if they received at least one grade in that subject area in eighth grade and at least one grade in that subject area in ninth grade. This excludes students who attended a charter school for the duration of either their eighth-grade or ninth-grade school year. For more information, see Appendix A.

five credits had a four-year graduation rate of just 44 percent. Of the seven credits most students attempt in ninth grade, only four or five are typically core credits—usually one credit each of math, English, science, and social studies. Therefore, the higher graduation rates for freshmen accumulating six and seven credits further underscore the importance of students' success in all their courses during freshman year, not just their core courses.

TABLE 1
Failures in Both Core- and Non-Core Courses in Ninth Grade Were Associated with Decreased Likelihood of Graduating from High School

Graduation Rate and Number of Students by Number of Core and Non-Core Course Failures in Ninth Grade, 2011-2014 Freshman Cohorts

		Core Failures			
		0	1	2	3+
Non-Core Failures	0	89.5% N=39,074	70.4% N=3,325	60.3% N=1,467	39.3% N=2,058
	1	67.6% N=1,901	58.1% N=881	49.1% N=652	23.6% N=1,916
	2	59.9% N=421	44.2% N=326	40.2% N=279	16.3% N=1,572
	3+	39.6% N=101	37.4% N=102	33.1% N=139	8.2% N=1,759

Note: Charter students were not included in this analysis because their freshman grades were not available. For more information, see Appendix A.

FIGURE 15
Students who Earned Seven Credits in Ninth Grade Were Twice as Likely to Graduate from High School as those who Earned Only Five Credits

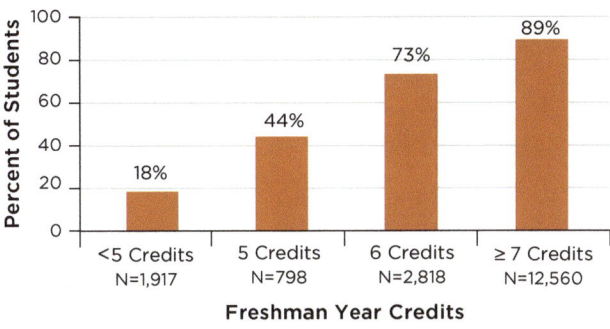

Graduation Rate by Number of Credits Accumulated During Freshman Year, 2013-14 Freshman Cohort

- <5 Credits (N=1,917): 18%
- 5 Credits (N=798): 44%
- 6 Credits (N=2,818): 73%
- ≥7 Credits (N=12,560): 89%

Note: Charter students were not included in this analysis because their freshman grades were not available. For more information, see Appendix A.

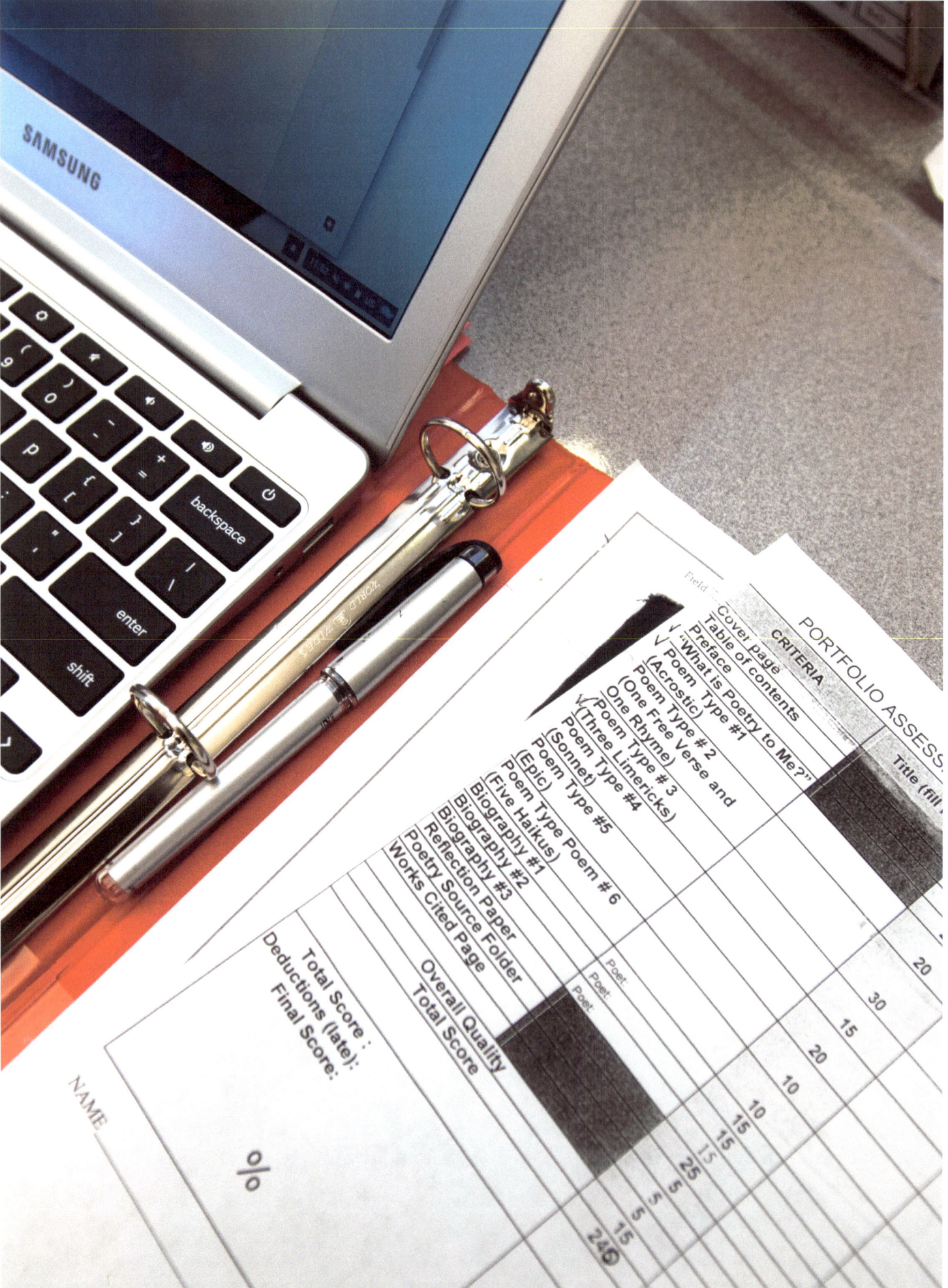

CHAPTER 4

Implications

Efforts to promote ninth-grade performance at CPS have been successful in improving outcomes for Chicago students, but continued declines in students' grades between eighth and ninth grade suggest a need for additional investment in the high school transition.

Over the past decade, CPS high schools have made significant progress in reducing core failures in ninth grade by closely monitoring students' progress in their core courses to ensure that they are receiving appropriate interventions and supports, and these efforts have resulted in large gains in Freshman OnTrack and high school graduation rates. However, from 2012–17, students' grades continued to decline in all subject areas between the eighth and ninth grades, including non-core subjects like arts and PE/health. Ninth-graders who earned high grades in the middle grades may not be at risk of falling off-track, but large declines in their overall GPAs between the eighth and ninth grades do have consequences for their access to selective colleges and their likelihood of earning a four-year degree.

Freshman success teams should be aware that even students with very high grades and attendance in eighth grade are at risk of grade declines in ninth grade. Many high-achieving Black and Latino students are not receiving the supports they need to make a successful transition to high school. Black students with the highest eighth-grade GPAs saw their core GPAs decline twice as much in ninth grade as their White peers with similar eighth-grade GPAs. The large GPA declines seen by the highest-achieving Black and Latino students are especially consequential because high school grades are a critical component of students' college access and college readiness. Only CPS graduates with a high school GPA above 2.5 have at least a 50 percent chance of enrolling in a four-year college.[25] Large GPA declines between the eighth and ninth grades put many Black and Latino ninth-graders who begin high school with a history of high academic achievement out of range for likely admission to selective colleges and universities, contributing to racial disparities in CPS students' college outcomes.

Non-core courses are as crucial for freshman success and longer-term success as core courses, and strategies to improve freshman performance could include all courses. All course failures in ninth grade, regardless of subject area, are important and it is in non-core classes that students saw the largest declines in GPA. The average freshman spends almost half of their school day in non-core courses, and their experiences in these classes shape their academic identity and how they engage in school.

Students' non-core grades also affect their ability to graduate from high school and their future access to selective and highly selective colleges. In this study, a failure in a non-core course was as detrimental to students' likelihood of graduating as a failure in a core

---

25 Roderick et al. (2006).

course, and low grades in the non-core subject areas affected graduates' GPAs just as much as low grades in the core subject areas. For the average CPS graduate, more than one-third of their cumulative graduating GPA was made up of grades in non-core courses.

Significant declines in non-core course performance between the eighth and ninth grades suggest that these subjects could also be incorporated into schools' efforts to promote freshman success. In order to ensure that students are receiving support in all of their courses, schools could include teachers in the non-core subject areas in Freshman Success meetings surrounding the supports that students may need in order to make a successful transition to high school.

Given the importance of freshman non-core courses, it may also be time to consider expanding the Freshman OnTrack metric to more fully reflect students' performance in all of their classes. Ninth-graders are currently considered to be on-track if they accumulate five credits by the end of their freshman year and fail, at most, one semester of a core course. Because most students are enrolled in seven credit-bearing courses during ninth grade, this means that ninth-graders who fail only one semester of a core course would be considered on-track even if they receive as many as three semester Fs in non-core courses, and ninth-graders who do not fail any core courses can be on-track if they receive as many as four semester Fs in non-core courses. Around 600 students each year fell into these categories in this study, earning a status of on-track despite receiving at least two total semester Fs during freshman year. These students were much less likely than other on-track students to graduate from high school: the students in this group in the 2013-14 freshman cohort had a four-year graduation rate of just 56 percent. Work around Freshman OnTrack has already contributed to great improvement in CPS students' performance and graduation rates across the district. Expanding the definition of the metric to include non-core failures could facilitate the inclusion of non-core teachers and departments in all freshman success work.

Large GPA declines and high failure rates for Black and Latino young men in the non-core subject areas in ninth grade, particularly in PE/health, suggest a need for additional review of non-core grading practices and standards. Because Freshman Success teams are generally made up of teachers in the core subject areas, teachers in PE/health, arts, and other non-core subject areas may have less exposure to messages about the importance of ninth-grade and the challenges their students may face during the transition to high school. Grading in the non-core subject areas may also be more likely than grading in the core subject areas to reflect teachers' expectations about student compliance and behavior. Further research could explore the role of grading practices and teacher bias in students' experiences and grades in PE/health and other non-core classes.

Patterns of GPA declines between the eighth and ninth grades varied significantly across high schools. Some high schools have become highly successful in maintaining or improving upon their incoming students' eighth-grade achievement, while other schools' freshmen continued to see significant declines across demographic and prior achievement categories. District-level disparities in students' ninth-grade grades raise important questions about inequities in students' experiences in ninth grade across the city, but they also mask considerable variation in these patterns across individual high schools. This variation suggests that school environment plays an important role in determining whether and how students' grades decline as they transition to ninth grade. In order to ensure that all students are reaching their full potential in ninth grade, all high schools could consider what additional supports their students might need in order to maintain or improve upon their achievement in the middle grades. Network and district leadership could also consider dedicating additional capacity and resources to supporting schools in this work.

References

Allensworth, E.M. (2013)
The use of ninth-grade early warning indicators to improve Chicago schools. *Journal of Education for Students Placed at Risk (JESPAR), 18*(1), 68-83.

Allensworth, E.M., & Clark, K. (2018)
Are GPAs an inconsistent measure of achievement across high schools? Examining assumptions about grades versus standardized test scores (Working Paper). Chicago, IL: University of Chicago Consortium on School Research.

Allensworth, E.M., Gwynne, J.A., Moore, P., & de la Torre, M. (2014)
Looking forward to high school and college: Middle grades indicators of readiness in Chicago Public Schools. Chicago, IL: University of Chicago Consortium on Chicago School Research.

Allensworth, E.M., Healey, K., Gwynne, J.A., & Crespin, R. (2016)
High school graduation rates through two decades of district change: The influence of policies, data records, and demographic shifts. Chicago, IL: University of Chicago Consortium on School Research.

Andrew, M., & Flashman. J. (2017)
School transitions, peer influence, and educational expectation formation: Girls and boys. *Social Science Research, 61*, 218-233.

Benner, A.D. (2011)
The transition to high school: Current knowledge, future directions. *Educational Psychology Review, 23*(3), 299-328.

Benner, A.D., & Graham, S. (2009)
The transition to high school as a developmental process among multiethnic urban youth. *Child Development, 80*(2), 356-376.

Bowen, W.G., Chingos, M.M., & McPherson, M.S. (2009)
Crossing the finish line: Completing college at America's public universities. Princeton, NJ: Princeton University Press.

Camara, W.J., & Echternacht, G. (2000)
The SAT[R] I and high school grades: Utility in predicting success in college. New York, NY: College Entrance Examination Board.

Easton, J.Q., Johnson, E., & Sartain, L. (2017)
The predictive power of ninth-grade GPA. Chicago, IL: University of Chicago Consortium on School Research.

Farrington, C.A., Roderick, M., Allensworth, E.M., Nagaoka, J., Keys, T.S., Johnson, D.W., & Beechum, N.O. (2012)
Teaching adolescents to become learners: The role of non-congnitive factors in shaping schools performance. Chicago, IL: University of Chicago Consortium on Chicago School Research.

Felmlee, D., McMillan, C., Rodis, P.I., & Osgood, D.W. (2018)
Falling behind: lingering costs of the high school transition for youth friendships and grades. *Sociology of Education, 91*(2), 159-182.

Geiser, S., & Santelices, V. (2007)
Validity of high school grades in predicting student success beyond the freshman year: High-school record versus standardized tests as indicators of four-year college outcomes. Berkeley, CA: University of Berkeley Center for Studies in Higher Education.

Nagaoka., J., Seeskin, A., & Coca, V.M. (2017)
The educational attainment of Chicago Public Schools students: 2016. Chicago, IL: University of Chicago Consortium on School Research.

Roderick, M., & Camburn, E. (1999)
Risk and recovery from course failure in the early years of high school. *American Educational Research Journal, 36*(2), 303-343.

Roderick, M., Kelley-Kemple, T., Johnson, D.W., & Beechum, N.O. (2014)
Preventable failure: Improvements in long-term outcomes when high schools focused on the ninth grade. Chicago, IL: University of Chicago Consortium on Chicago School Research.

Roderick M., Nagaoka, J., & Allensworth, E. (2006)
From high school to the future: A first look at Chicago public school graduates' college enrollment, college preparation, and graduation from four-year colleges. Chicago, IL: University of Chicago Consortium on Chicago School Research.

Rosenkranz, T., de la Torre, M., Stevens, W.D., & Allensworth, E.M. (2014)
Free to fail or on-track to college: Why grades drop when students enter high school and what adults can do about it. Chicago, IL: University of Chicago Consortium on Chicago School Research.

Appendix A
Data Decisions

For the purposes of this analysis, the 2016 freshman cohort was defined as the students who were enrolled in the ninth grade at CPS high schools for the first time during the 2016–17 school year. Students were included in the sample only if they were enrolled in the eighth grade at a CPS school in May 2016 and in the ninth grade at a CPS school in October 2016, and only if they had a calculable GPA for at least one semester of both school years. Because of limited data availability, students who were enrolled in a CPS charter school for the duration of either the 2015–16 or 2016–17 school year (or both) are excluded.[26] Charter school students constituted 27 percent of first-time ninth-graders in the 2016–17 cohort. However, the sample did include grades from schools of several other types, including neighborhood high schools, selective enrollment high schools, and selective academic centers for middle grade students. Of the 2016 freshman cohort, 15,914 students satisfied these criteria. Inclusion rules for earlier cohorts mirrored those used for the 2016 freshman cohort.

Thoughout this report, "core GPA" refers to grade point averages of core courses: math, English, science, and social studies. "Grades" refer to individual course grades (semester or year). For analyses involving individual subject areas, grades were averaged first at the student level. For each subject area in the analysis, average grades included only students who received at least one grade in that subject area in eighth grade and at least one grade in that subject area in ninth grade. Each student is included once, at most, for each subject, regardless of how many grades they received in that subject area. Grades awarded in core, arts, and PE/health courses comprised 88 percent of all grades awarded in the eighth grade and 77 percent of all grades awarded in the ninth grade.

---

[26] Many CPS charter schools use different student information systems from the IMPACT system used by non-charter schools. Because each system varies in the way that it stores information about courses, credits, teachers, periods, grades, and other data, creating linkages across systems is difficult, and our data archive currently does not include records of charter school students' course performance.

Appendix B
GPAs and Failure Rates by Subject Area and Subgroup

TABLE B.1

Average Eighth-Grade GPAs of 2016–17 Ninth-Graders, by Core GPA Category and Subject Area

GPA Category	Core	Arts	PE/Health
3.5-4.0	3.83	3.91	3.94
3.0-3.5	3.2	3.69	3.82
2.0-3.0	2.49	3.35	3.61
<2.0	1.41	2.85	3.26

Note: For each subject area, students are included only if they received at least one grade in that subject area in eighth grade during school year 2015–16 and at least one grade in that subject area in ninth grade during school year 2016–17. This excludes students who attended a charter school for the duration of either their eighth- or ninth-grade school year. For more information, see Appendix A.

TABLE B.2

Average Eighth-Grade GPAs of 2016–17 Ninth-Graders, by Race/Ethnicity and Gender in Different Subject Areas

Race/Ethnicity & Gender	Core	Arts	PE/Health
White Young Men	3.03	3.64	3.80
White Young Women	3.44	3.90	3.89
Latino Young Men	2.64	3.39	3.71
Latino Young Women	3.10	3.72	3.77
Black Young Men	2.46	3.20	3.57
Black Young Women	2.92	3.58	3.58
Asian Young Men	3.14	3.73	3.85
Asian Young Women	3.49	3.55	3.71

Note: For each subject area, students were included only if they received at least one grade in that subject area in eighth grade during school year 2015–16 and at least one grade in that subject area in ninth grade during school year 2016–17. This excludes students who attended a charter school for the duration of either their eighth- or ninth-grade school year. For more information, see Appendix A.

TABLE B.3

Eighth- and Ninth-Grade Failure Rates by Subject Area, 2012-13 Freshman Cohort

Subject	Number of 9th-Graders	Students with Failures (8th)	Students with Failures (9th)	Percent with Failures (8th)	Percent with Failures (9th)
English	18,123	1,795	2,822	9.9%	15.6%
Math	17,838	968	3,004	5.4%	16.8%
Science	17,847	1,368	2,654	7.7%	14.9%
Social Studies	16,474	983	2,421	6.0%	14.7%
Arts	8,305	143	748	1.7%	9.0%
PE/Health	17,192	176	2,282	1.0%	13.3%
Core	18,162	3,030	4,966	16.7%	27.3%

Note: For each subject area, students were included only if they received at least one grade in that subject area in eighth grade during school year 2011–12 and at least one grade in that subject area in the ninth grade during school year 2012–13. This excludes students who attended a charter school for the duration of either their eighth- or ninth-grade school year. For more information, see Appendix A.

TABLE B.4

Eighth- and Ninth-Grade Failure Rates by Subject area, 2016-17 Freshman Cohort

Subject	Number of 9th-Graders	Students with Failures (8th)	Students with Failures (9th)	Percent with Failures (8th)	Percent with Failures (9th)
English	15,855	738	1,390	4.7%	8.8%
Math	15,371	317	1,503	2.1%	9.8%
Science	15,680	413	1,335	2.6%	8.5%
Social Studies	15,435	346	1,206	2.2%	7.8%
Arts	8,693	97	614	1.1%	7.1%
PE/Health	15,453	69	1,289	0.4%	8.3%
Core	15,914	1,152	2,688	7.2%	16.9%

Note: For each subject area, students were included only if they received at least one grade in that subject area in eighth grade during school year 2015–16 and at least one grade in that subject area in ninth grade during school year 2016–17. This excludes students who attended a charter school for the duration of either their eighth- or ninth-grade school year. For more information, see Appendix A.

ABOUT THE AUTHORS

ALEX SEESKIN is the Chief Strategy Officer at the Urban Education Institute (UEI) where he is responsible for guiding strategy for the organization and leading high priority work across and within UEI's units. Seeskin also the leads To&Through Project (toandthrough.uchicago.edu), which aims to empower educators and families with research, data, and resources they need to move more students to and through high school and college. Previously, he served as the Director of Strategy of UChicago Charter, and as a resident at UChicago Impact. Prior to coming to UEI, Seeskin taught high school English in Chicago Public Schools for seven years, serving as the English Department Chair at Lake View High School from 2008-12. Seeskin earned a BS in communications from Northwestern University and an EdLD from Harvard University.

JENNY NAGAOKA is the Deputy Director of the UChicago Consortium, where she has conducted research for over 20 years. Her research interests focus on policy and practice in urban education reform, particularly using data to connect research and practice and examining the school environments and instructional practices that promote college readiness and success. She has co-authored numerous journal articles and reports, including studies of college readiness, noncognitive factors, the transition from high school to post-secondary education, and authentic intellectual instruction. She is the lead researcher on the To&Through Project, a project that provides educators, policymakers, and families with research, data, and training on the milestones that matter most for college success. Nagaoka is the lead author of *Foundations for Young Adult Success: A Developmental Framework* (2015), which draws on research and practice evidence to build a coherent framework of the foundational factors for young adult success and investigates their development from early childhood through young adulthood and how they can be supported through developmental experiences and relationships. Nagaoka received her BA from Macalester College and her master's degree in public policy from the Irving B. Harris School of Public Policy at the University of Chicago.

SHELBY MAHAFFIE is a Research Analyst at the UChicago Consortium on School Research. In this role, she conducts data analysis for the To&Through Project, which provides educators and families with data and research on improving students' college access and attainment. Prior to joining the Consortium, she worked as a research assistant at the University of Chicago Urban Labs, where she contributed to research on youth employment and workforce development programs in Chicago. Mahaffie received her BA in economics and public policy from the University of Chicago.

This report reflects the interpretation of the authors. Although the UChicago Consortium's Steering Committee provided technical advice, no formal endorsement by these individuals or organizations, nor the full Consortium or the To&Through Project, should be assumed.

UCHICAGO Consortium on School Research

Directors

ELAINE M. ALLENSWORTH
Lewis-Sebring Director

CAMILLE A. FARRINGTON
Managing Director and Senior Research Associate

HOLLY HART
Survey Director

KYLIE KLEIN
Director of Research Operations

BRONWYN MCDANIEL
Director of Outreach and Communication

JENNY NAGAOKA
Deputy Director

MELISSA RODERICK
*Senior Director
Hermon Dunlap Smith Professor
School of Social Service Administration*

PENNY BENDER SEBRING
Co-Founder

MARISA DE LA TORRE
Managing Director and Senior Research Associate

Steering Committee

RAQUEL FARMER-HINTON
Co-Chair
University of Wisconsin, Milwaukee

LUISIANA MELÉNDEZ
Co-Chair
Erikson Institute

Institutional Members

SARAH DICKSON
Chicago Public Schools

ELIZABETH KIRBY
Chicago Public Schools

TROY LARAVIERE
Chicago Principals and Administrators Association

JESSE SHARKEY
Chicago Teachers Union

TONY SMITH
Illinois State Board of Education

Individual Members

KATHLEEN CALIENTO
The Academy Group

GINA CANEVA
Lindblom Math & Science

NANCY CHAVEZ
OneGoal

JAHMAL COLE
My Block, My Hood, My City

KATIE HILL
Office of the Cook County State's Attorney

MEGAN HOUGARD
Chicago Public Schools

GREG JONES
The Academy Group

PRANAV KOTHARI
Revolution Impact, LLC

AMANDA LEWIS
University of Illinois at Chicago

RITO MARTINEZ
Surge Institute

SHAZIA MILLER
NORC at the University of Chicago

MICHELLE MORALES
Mikva Challenge

CRISTINA PACIONE-ZAYAS
Erikson Institute

BEATRIZ PONCE DE LEÓN
Generation All

PAIGE PONDER
One Million Degrees

REBECCA VONDERLACK-NAVARRO
Latino Policy Forum

Pam Witmer
Office of the Mayor, City of Chicago

JOHN ZEIGLER
DePaul University

www.ingramcontent.com/pod-product-compliance
Lightning Source LLC
Chambersburg PA
CBHW041542040426
42446CB00002B/198